I0474100

"HELP...
I'm Addicted To
Internet
Marketing!"

Will You Be Too?

www.RandolfSmith.com

© 2011 by *RandolfSmith.com*

All rights reserved.

All Rights Reserved. No part of this publication may be reproduced in any form or by any means, including scanning, photocopying, or otherwise without prior written permission of the copyright holder.

Disclaimer and Terms of Use: The Author and Publisher has strived to be as accurate and complete as possible in the creation of this book, notwithstanding the fact that he does not warrant or represent at any time that the contents within are accurate due to the rapidly changing nature of the Internet. While all attempts have been made to verify information provided in this publication, the Author and Publisher assumes no responsibility for errors, omissions, or contrary interpretation of the subject matter herein. Any perceived slights of specific persons, peoples, or organizations are unintentional. In practical advice books, like anything else in life, there are no guarantees of income made. Readers are cautioned to reply on their own judgment about their individual circumstances to act accordingly. This book is not intended for use as a source of legal, business, accounting or financial advice. All readers are advised to seek services of competent professionals in legal, business, accounting, and finance field.

First Printing, 2011

ISBN-13:
978-1468031973

ISBN-10:
146803197X

Printed in the United States of America Written in UK English ☺

Dedication

I'd like to dedicate this book to all the people who have supported me in my addiction.
Family, Friends and online colleagues, as well as all the people who will in the future by reading my rambles and connecting with me both online and off.

That includes YOU dear reader.
I sincerely wish you every success, and hope you too can enjoy a life filled with passion... and are able to pass that passion on to future generations

"HELP! ...
I'M ADDICTED TO
INTERNET
MARKETING!"

By

Randy Smith
www.RandolfSmith.com

Will You Be TOO?

Table of Contents

I'M ADDICTED TO INTERNET MARKETING!

Today, I'm going public and letting everyone know what I do for a living, along with admitting my addictions, which I've kept secret for the past several years.

But first, I need to get this out into the open.

My Name is Randolf Smith and **I'm an Internet Marketer!**

My family, friends, and the people I come in contact with everyday seem to have a difficult time understanding what I do when I say I'm an Internet Marketer. Quite frankly, they wonder how I make my money, and I'm sure some think that I'm surviving on a trust fund or inheritance or possibly something illegal! *(laughing)*

Trying to tell someone what I do can become quite difficult because it's not as simple as saying I'm a replacement window salesman, or I sell insurance. That's why I decided to write this book, and maybe the same reasons that I had for becoming an Internet Marketer will appeal to you,too.

What is an Internet Marketer?

When you're involved in Internet marketing, you're a virtual sales person who can sell or advertise anything, to anyone, anywhere, as long as your customer has Internet access. You don't need a storefront; all you need is an Internet connection and a computer, or electronic device. When you market your products and services on the Internet, you can be called an Internet Marketer. You can even be an Internet Marketer and still have a full-time job.

Some people confuse Internet marketing (known as IM) with Multi-Level Marketing (MLM), because they often grimace and say something like, "I'm not into that pyramid buying stuff." At that point, I explain that I'm an ethical Internet marketer, and I'm not into MLM, nor do I scam people for a living.

Many MLM companies start off by selling you one product, and then they give you an income opportunity. That just means that you can "buy" your way into a sales level or position, and usually the more money you pay results in more perks, benefits, or higher profits and earning levels. That's not what Internet Marketing is.

Take eBay, Amazon, Etsy, or any number of organizations that allow you to set up an account, and then you can sell products through their Internet business. As long as you're not just selling something for a one-time sale, then each of the above are examples of Internet Marketing.

But IM is much more than that. It's marketing a product or service using the Internet that can attract customers that you could never reach with a brick-and-mortar business. Marketing through the Internet opens up a vast world of customers that have the potential to buy your product without ever having met you.

Have you ever ordered something from a company on the Internet?

Maybe the owner placed an ad that you clicked on, or you found the company by typing words into your browser for a specific product.

Sometimes your Internet Marketing products will consist of information that an online customer is seeking as a quick download. At other times, people might want a physical product that you'd ship to them. In both instances, if you gave that business your name and email address, it's possible that you received a follow-up email or offer, and then a third offer, and so forth.

Now that's Internet Marketing—selling information and products on the Internet to someone over and over again. As long as you've joined their mailing list, you'll continue to receive their offers. In essence, once you've bought something from that company, you're more likely to buy from them again. **Now imagine if you had a business like that.**

My First Steps to Becoming an Internet Marketing Addict

For years I wanted an independent lifestyle, which meant I dreamt of having a job where I would work for myself, instead of making someone else rich. I wanted flexibility and the right to decide when I would work and where I would work. I wanted to wake up every morning knowing that I was making enough money to support myself and my family, or at least provide a valuable income stream to give ourselves more choices in life.

I dreamed of the day when I would look out my window in the morning and see the sun shining and that it was OKAY not to work that day. I wanted to give myself permission to take off whenever I felt the urge, fully recognizing that I needed to be accountable to my new business demands.

I had heard that Internet Marketers *(IMers)* worked part-time and made a full-time income. I also learned that many IMers make more money in six months than many professionals make in one year. I wanted to be one of those statistics. I was willing to work extra hours each day, in addition to my other responsibilities, just to make that happen. You must admit that's a commitment!

During the many months of putting in lots of hours at my computer and striving for my dream of quitting my full-time job, I became obsessed with learning about Internet

Marketing. Those big famous gurus all made it sound so easy.

A Little about Me and How I Knew I Was Becoming an IM Addict

I thought I knew what I was doing, and I thought I had set my goals appropriately, but somewhere in time, I began spending money on IM courses, tools, software, and any product that I knew **I JUST HAD TO HAVE FOR MY BUSINESS!**

Yes, I was addicted to buying every new thing that someone marketed to me. The process of buying information for my business had me spending my entire IM budget just to get my hands on the next deal that was sure to make me successful. The point is that I was willing to do the work, and I knew that there was no magic button to press that would make me an instant millionaire.

The problem was that I was buying so many deals that I hadn't even considered that I'd never use 99 percent of them. It was as if my mind tricked me into thinking that the dime-sale price *(where the product price increases by a fixed amount after a specific number of sales)* would never be lower and I had to buy it RIGHT NOW!

It was euphoric buying each product. I was excited and filled with adrenaline knowing that I had gotten in early and was paying a decent price. But then in one instance, before I was sent to the download page, I was presented with another offer, but it cost much more than the item I had just purchased.

As I sat there anxiously waiting to see what was inside the download area, I read and re-read the second *offer (sometimes called an OTO, a one time offer or upsell)*, and the way everything was worded I suddenly felt like I couldn't make a decision.

Should I leave the page and just get the link to download the product I bought?
But what if I really needed the add-on product to be successful?

I couldn't decide, but I didn't want to miss the chance to buy the add-on at the low price, so I bought it. I didn't even consider how much I had spent. I just knew I HAD to have it. That's kind of when I knew I was an Internet Marketing addict.

For an hour I felt so happy and lucky that I got such a sweet deal from one of the top Internet Marketers. I just knew in my heart that I could make $5,000 this month, as long as I had the time on the weekend to read the report or follow the videos and implement the steps. The sales copy had sounded so convincing!

But by the time the weekend rolled around, I had bought ten other products that I just "knew" were as good if not better than the one I had purchased earlier in the week.

You'd think by that point that I would have known I was addicted to buying every new product, course, report or video series, but I didn't even give it a second thought.

On the weekend, my friends invited me to come over, and I couldn't resist the idea of getting away and enjoying their company. By Monday morning, I was headed to my job. I again thought that I really should set some time aside to read at least one of the reports from beginning to end. How else could I "commit" to doing something if I didn't take action? **I reminded myself that doing nothing produces nothing**. I had to get motivated and take action. My dream of becoming an Internet Marketer was still alive.

However, true to my addictive state, I couldn't resist reading all the offers that found their way into my Inbox; and then there were my favourite forums. I would cruise the offers on three forums every single evening after work. I convinced myself that I was doing research, and in some regards, I was. Yet by the world's standards, I was in denial.

Before heading off to bed one night, I read this in one of the reports I bought:

"To succeed in any program, make sure that you're buying into something that you believe in and you think is achievable. Then set a goal to take action implementing one phase of that product within 24 hours following your purchase. Next, promise yourself that you will take at least one additional action during the

upcoming week that furthers the launch of the product you just bought. If you can't commit to those rules, then cut up your credit cards so you can't buy anything else."

I promised myself that I'd take action within one week.

My First Sale as an Internet Marketer

I still remember the first time I got home from my full-time job and opened my email program. There it was—notification of my first sale. Wow! I felt like I had just won the lottery, well, not from the money perspective, but from the shock and surprise that something I did had actually paid off. That one sale is what encouraged me to learn as much as I could about Internet Marketing.

I still put in a lot of long hours sitting at the computer. For me, it's personally satisfying to work on a new revenue stream, an information product, or creating a service that I know others need. But very often, well, most of the time, actually, my social life gets put on hold and the people in my life don't always appreciate being in second place. But when you're first getting started in Internet Marketing, I found that taking action was the only thing that was my path for making that first sale.

My advice, if you're thinking about getting into Internet Marketing is this: **Don't say you're going to TRY it! Say you're going to COMMIT to it.**

Just remember that time management will become a priority in your life. As with any dream, you have to pace yourself and set realistic goals. One thing is for sure—if you think it will take you five hours to do something meaningful in your business, double that time. Then you won't get discouraged if it takes you longer than you estimated or that someone told you it would take.

The more I learn about Internet Marketing and all the ways there are of earning an income, the more I get addicted to it.

People Notice When You Love What You Do

I'll bet if you asked 10 random people on the street if they absolutely LOVED their job, you'd be doing well if even one of those 10 people said yes. Most people complain about their jobs, even those who are earning top pay. If you're lucky, you get two weeks paid vacation and maybe you get paid for several holidays during the year. Nevertheless, in these days of economic challenges, many workers are just grateful that they have a J.O.B.

Becoming an Internet Marketing Addict requires taking risks and putting in long hours before you achieve your goal of living out your life's dream and passion.

The beautiful part about becoming an Internet Marketer is that when you've achieved your success, everything else in your life feels like a luxury. You wake up every morning knowing that the market you've chosen to target is one that you're totally passionate about. When you love what you do, people notice.

Requirements for Becoming an Internet Marketer

Internet marketing success doesn't depend upon your background or previous work experiences. I've known high school and college students, housewives, grandmothers, drug addicts, people living on welfare, and corporate world geniuses who have made six-figure incomes as an Internet Marketer. The secret to becoming an Internet Marketer is that if you can follow a course, a blueprint, or read up on the various topics of Internet Marketing online that are free, and implement IM methods, and don't quit, you'll make money.

The secret phrase is "Take Action." If you don't take action, you won't achieve your dream. No one is going to hand you an IM business on a silver platter, all done for you, unless you take the action to "keep on keeping on!"

Yes, you can make a very decent living as an Internet Marketer, if you put in the time to make it work. If you quit before making your first $100, and move onto buying the next shiny object, then you'll be less inclined to make enough money to go full-time.

INCOME STREAM CHOICES FOR INTERNET MARKETERS

Starting an Internet Marketing business requires that you spend money initially on two things: a computer and a monthly fee for Internet connectivity. To add two more bare essentials, you would then consider a web hosting account ($10/month) and an email marketing account ($20/month). Just so that you're not misled, it's best if you can afford an additional $100/month for advertising or even outsourcing a writer to create content for your website or for article marketing.

Successful Internet Marketers will tell you that you can sell products and services to any consumer in the entire world, as long as you've identified that the marketplace has a demand for the specific niche product you want to sell. However, you have no geographical boundaries as an Internet Marketer. Find a hungry market, either local or online, and you can sell them something and make money.

Should You Select One Income Stream or Several?

I've found that it's best to start your Internet Marketing career staying focused on one income stream until you're starting to make some money with it. Then move on to adding a second stream, and then a third, always increasing the profit to your bottom line.

Many IMers will tell you that you shouldn't put all your efforts into just one revenue stream, because if one method collapses within a niche market or dries up, you stand a chance of losing a lot of money. When you select multiple revenue streams, you're protecting your investment of time and dollars. If one income method ends, you still have several more to rely upon, which will keep your status as an Internet Marketer, and not force you back into working for someone else.

As a side note, one of my mentors always says **"Many Streams Make A River!"** I learned the hard way not to put all my eggs in one basket after a hacking incident that lost me 80% of my online income streams overnight back in 2010.

Many Internet Marketers start their new business by creating a website with a keyword-rich domain name, and from that site they can begin selling information products that can be downloaded. Then maybe they branch out into selling niche market physical products such as T-shirts, mugs for special events, and so forth.

Other income streams include affiliate marketing, writing, and selling eBooks, and writing articles and selling them to niche markets for website content or marketing purposes. While still other avenues of generating an income are through blogging, ghostwriting, creating mobile websites, building and flipping WordPress sites, selling backlinks, creating videos and Facebook Fan pages, setting up social media accounts, and even selling Search Engine Optimization, or SEO, services.

One of the most important aspects to know is that the majority of Internet Marketers make money by selling information. **Let's look at that income stream first as a way to get started.**

CREATING AND SELLING INFORMATION PRODUCTS

Information products provide customers with instant information dedicated to a specific topic. Internet marketers call these niche markets. When people want information fast, they search the Internet by typing in a string of words that will return a list of websites that talk about the topic. Information that is easily available online, however, might take web surfing time of two to three hours to give you the answers you're looking for.

Since the information you want most often seems to be incomplete, that's because the facts are scattered throughout many websites, and it's up to you to compile your own information. But what if the information someone was searching for online was available in a short report, eBook, or as an audio file that could be downloaded immediately?

Most likely the person searching for the information would spend a small amount of money just to have the ability to immediately download and access all the information that an author had put together.

As an Internet marketer, you can compile the research data within a specific niche market and release your own special report or eBook for sale. By doing so, you will create a product once, but you will be able to sell it hundreds or thousands of times. If you choose an evergreen topic *(information that is true today and will still be true many years into the future)*, your product will not go out of date. This means that you can make money over and over again.

What Should You Write About?

Finding a topic that will interest many people sometimes creates a stumbling block for brand-new Internet marketers. They think they have to have just the most perfect niche with the most perfect title, in the most perfect demanding marketplace. That's not true.

Perhaps you're just getting started in Internet marketing, or maybe you've been at this for a while. One quick way to find out what customers are looking for is to page through magazines that you might have at home or at your office. Every magazine is a target niche market. Choosing evergreen topics such as health, family, relationships, money, or a specific hobby or craft will always be in-demand target markets.

There are two types of people who you can write for: other Internet Marketers or Consumers who will gladly pay for the information you provide. You can share secrets, blueprints, strategies, and step-by-step instructions for how to do almost anything. If you can talk, you can write.

<u>Here's a tip</u>:

Hire a professional editor or proofreader to correct your spelling and grammar before publishing your writing. It's not very expensive, and it will make your product look professional.

If you're short on cash, you might want to consider offering a free copy of your book in exchange for someone's proofreading expertise.

What If You're Not an Expert on the Topic You Want To Write About?

You don't have to be an expert on every topic that you write about and every eBook that you release for sale. You can research any topic online for free. You can visit forums and read what others are talking about to get detailed information to use in your book. You can interview someone and create a book out of the interview, complete with questions and answers that go along with your commentary.

The secret to creating an information product that will sell well is to provide good, solid information in an easy to understand format. By making it appealing to your target audience, if they like what you wrote in one book, they'll most likely want to buy your next book, providing it's in the same target market.

If you have a great sense of humour when someone meets you in person, then make sure to include humour in your writing style. Just remember to keep the writing professional, which means get rid of curse words or anything that would negatively impact a specific group of people.

Many Internet Marketers make their living through writing, others through their graphic design skills, some create their own software, and others make a living through blogging. Just as there are many careers for people to choose from in the offline world, there are multiple ways to make your living following the Internet Marketing career path.

However, everything that you do as an Internet Marketer will involve some type of writing, whether it's creating info products, creating web content, writing an emotional sales letter, or writing ads and answering emails; your personality and your passion will come across in all your communications with your customers and fellow Internet Marketers. Sometimes that's all it takes for people to buy a product from you.

Write Your Own Content or Hire a Writer?

It's not just a matter of flipping a coin to decide what you're going to do. If you are a fast writer and you enjoy writing, then write the first product yourself. If you don't like to write, or you don't feel that your spelling and grammar can measure up to a professional product, then you might want to hire a freelance writer or a ghostwriter.

A ghostwriter is someone that you pay to do the writing for you. Essentially, you create the title and the chapter headings. You find out how much a writer will charge, either as a flat fee for a number of pages, or at a per-word rate.

Some Internet Marketers are very qualified writers, but they have full-time jobs that are very demanding. If they had to rely on writing their own names into their schedule to create an information product, they might not be very productive. You can do an online search for a ghostwriter or a freelance writer. Or, you can check in any of the forums that you might belong to and see if someone would be willing to give you a quote for the type of product or writing that you want to create.

Finding a writer who understands what you're trying to convey through your product might take several tries, but it's not difficult once you know the type of writer you're looking for and the price you want to pay.

Just remember that if your target audience is English-speaking people, your writer should be able to convey words, expressions, and use grammar that is correct for the language. If you're not familiar with sentence structure, grammar, and punctuation, then you might need to ask a family member or friend to give it a read before publishing it. Again, editors and proofreaders are more than happy to help turn your manuscript into a professional document that you can sell for years to come.

Turning One Information Product Into Several Products

Imagine for a moment that you have created one special report that you have converted into a PDF file that anyone can download for the price you set. You start making sales selling that one product, but before creating your second product for an additional income stream, you should think about creating multiple products.

Why? You've already done all the work to locate, research, and write the information that will help others. Now you can take that same information and convert it into multiple products. You can sell those products separately at their own prices, or you can combine all the products together to create one giant home study course. Naturally, the big bundle would sell for a lot more money than just one downloadable PDF file.

Below is a short list of products that you can create as an offshoot of your original information product:

- **Create an audio version**. Using free tools that you can download online, you would read the information contained inside your product and create an MP3 file. You can sell the MP3 file for a separate price as an immediate download, and you can also burn the MP3 file to a CD and sell it as a physical product. A great free tool you can use is called Audacity and is available for download at www.audacity.sourceforge.net/. Audacity can't save MP3 files without a plug-in. This plug-in is, however, available on Audacity's download page – not hidden off in some obscure corner of the web.

- **Create a "Top 10" PowerPoint presentation**. The top 10 is a list of items that the information seeker would find extremely helpful that go along with the product. This could be the top 10 advantages, the top 10 tips, top 10 solutions to a problem, etc.

- **Create a video using your PowerPoint presentation**. Upload it to online video sites as well as displaying it on your website as a teaser for the full-blown product.

- **Create 10 articles from the information you gathered**. Submit the articles to article directories, or use the articles on your website as content.

- **Rewrite those 10 articles and sell them as a Private Label Rights (PLR) pack**. Private label rights products give customers permission to revise your product and put their name on it.

- **Create a webinar** using a portion of what is in your information product with a call-to-action at the end of the webinar asking your attendees to buy your information product at a discount.

- **Summarize the information product and offer it as a free giveaway** after someone signs up for your mailing list with a link to purchase the full version.

Internet Marketers make a substantial amount of money by creating and selling information products. You probably won't have to do much searching on the Internet to find downloadable books that teach you how to create information products.

However, if you're on a budget, you can locate all the information yourself and arrange it into a document that can easily be converted to a PDF file, which, in essence, is a downloadable report or eBook. No trees have been sacrificed to print your eBook or report. It's a digital file that anyone can download to their computer or portable device.

When you're selling a downloadable product, there are no shipping costs, and your customer receives instant gratification knowing that within minutes after they've paid they will be directed to a download link and can instantly begin reading your report.

Remember, just by creating a product one time, you can sell it thousands of times. To get started, after your information product has been created, add a link after your signature in your email account announcing a first look, or a giveaway to a portion of your product. Include this link in every email you send out. People are curious. If the topic interests them, they'll click your link.

In case you're wondering how people will pay you, it's easy to set up a PayPal account at http://www.paypal.com.

After you have registered for a PayPal account, and you have logged in, all you have to do is click the help button at the top right side of the page, and you will see step-by-step tutorials that show you how to do anything, including putting the "Buy Now" button on your website so that you can sell your information product.

PayPal, along with other third-party payment providers, make it easy for Internet marketers to sell their products, and it makes it easy for customers to click a button and download their product. The need for information is immediate, and when you provide immediate download capability for your products, you'll meet your customer's needs: I WANT IT NOW!

Your customer won't have to drive to their local bookstore or place an online order and wait days until it arrives. That also means that the customer does not have to pay for shipping, and your product is available 24 hours a day. As an Internet Marketer you don't even have to be in your office or at home to sell something. See how addicting this can get?

Finding Ways to Market and Advertise Your Information Product

At the beginning of your Internet Marketing career, your most important step is to try something and take action. If you decide to create and sell an information product, you can create a one-page sales letter that talks about your product and includes a payment button and instructions for the buyer, telling them what to do to get your product.

You can advertise your product on your website; you can promote it through your blog, and you can advertise it in your signature file for every email that you send out. The trick is to discover which marketing and advertising tactic brings in the most sales. You can also sell your eBook through eBook directories or affiliate networks. Basically, you list your product with them, you decide how much to charge, and then you monitor the traffic and the sales.

If you belong to a forum where the members would be interested in the product that you have to sell, you can either create a classified ad or you can write classified ads on free sites with a link pointing back to your website where customers can purchase your product.

One of the best ways to market and advertise any products that you create is to have an email marketing sign-up form on your website. When a visitor arrives at your website or blog, your sign-up box should offer something in exchange for them to give you their email address. Then in a series of emails you can drip feed important information to them without asking them to buy something, at least for the first couple emails.

Then you can add new content to your website and include a link to the book that you're selling. Encourage the subscribers on your list to read more about it; then include the link that takes them directly to your website. This accomplishes two things: it brings more traffic to your website, and it gives you an opportunity to say more about the product you're selling outside of an email.

Certainly there are many products on the market that talk about traffic, marketing, and advertising products, and you might be attracted to buying those information packets at the beginning of your IM career. The best advice is to try something and see if you get a few sales.

<u>NOTE</u>: This is where the Internet Marketer addict side of you could potentially take over. Beware of buying every product that you hear about before first trying one method to see if it works for you.

MEMBERSHIP SITES

Another revenue stream that many successful Internet Marketers swear by is membership sites. The way that you make money through a membership site is by selling subscriptions. Members sign up by paying a recurring fee for every month that they remain a subscriber.

Membership sites can be set up to sell eBooks, Private Label Rights articles, website graphics, website templates, WordPress themes, video templates, autoresponder messages, and even coaching and mentoring services. As long as the membership site continues to add new content and/or products every month and the members are happy with the quality offered, you could have recurring income for an indefinite amount of time.

Setting up your own membership site doesn't take long if you have an easy to install membership script or software that allows members to login to their account. It's easy to start off with an inexpensive membership solution and then when you have accumulated extra money, you can upgrade to a more robust system.

Three of the best wordpress membership plugins available are :

www.digitalaccesspass.com/, www.yourmembers.co.uk/ and www.s2member.com/ .

Advantages for the Internet Marketer

The advantage of having a membership site is that you have a captive audience for your products. When the products are created they are uploaded and ready to allow subscribers to access them. Membership site subscriptions can range in price depending on the type of content provided to its members.

Some membership sites only sell their products to people who have signed up for private access, or other sites may sell the same information if they have access to PLR. One thing is certain; no two membership sites are the same even if they're selling similar content.

By having a list of members who have subscribed to a membership site, the site owner can send out periodic newsletters letting the subscribers know that new content has been added.

Depending upon the type of membership site software that you have installed, products can be available during only one month and then subscribers would have to pay extra money to purchase previous archived products. Or, everything that is put into the membership area stays there until the site owner removes it. You can make your own rules and decide what is best for yourself and for your members.

Most membership site software or scripts also have a method for automatically generating a lost password or username, thus, the subscriber wouldn't have to contact you. Dealing with support issues is your responsibility and at one time or another you will most likely have to step in and help one of your subscribers log in or download a product. This is normal for an Internet Marketer. If you respond quickly to support requests, you will find favour with your subscribers.

Membership sites are just one way that Internet Marketers make a lot of money. Let's talk about affiliate marketing as another income stream.

AFFILIATE MARKETING

Affiliate marketing is a marketing practice in which a business rewards one or more affiliates for each visitor or customer brought to their site through the affiliate's marketing efforts. Examples include reward sites, where users are rewarded with cash or gifts, for the completion of an offer, and the referral of others to the site.

The affiliate marketing industry has four core players: the merchant *(also known as the retailer or brand),* the network, the publisher *(also known as the affiliate),* and the customer. The market has grown in complexity and some affiliate marketing sites will have a secondary tier of players, including affiliate management agencies, super-affiliates and specialized third-party vendors.

Affiliate marketing overlaps with other Internet Marketing methods to some degree, because affiliates often use regular advertising methods, such as organic search engine optimization, email marketing, paid search engine marketing, and display advertising.

Use Creativity for Attracting Customers to Your Affiliate Offers

Affiliate marketers prosper through creative ways of getting customers to an affiliate offer so that they can make a commission. To protect the consumer, you might see a disclaimer at the lower portion of an affiliate marketer's email message that basically says the email could contain a link to an affiliate site and if you click that link, the Internet Marketer will receive a commission. Not every Internet Marketer reveals that they're promoting an affiliate's product.

You can become an affiliate marketer through a private business owner's affiliate program, or you can search for affiliate or partner programs offered by thousands of retailers. The unique way of generating an income stream through affiliate marketing is that you are not required to have your own product.

If you can direct people to a specific website and they buy something as a result of your recommendation or suggestion, then you've just made a sale. The smart Internet Marketer will try to capture the customer's name and email address before sending that person to the affiliate's website.

Affiliates Bring Increased Revenue to Companies

Any company or business who has an online shopping presence realizes that affiliates continue to play a significant role in their marketing strategies. To the average shopper who is unaware of online buying perks, that person may not be aware that you're making a commission after they buy something through your link.

If you've ever purchased something online and were redirected to a thank you page where you could download your product, you might have seen a second offer, a recommended product, or a bonus download. All of these are marketing tactics that an Internet Marketer can use to bring you information that you may not otherwise have heard about.

Companies and businesses, regardless if they're a one-person shop or have multiple locations around the world, know that by having an affiliate program, their sales will increase. As an affiliate marketer, you can direct your customers to an affiliate offer, and when they purchase, you make a commission. The company's happy, and you're happy to have made a sale.

Affiliate Commission Payment Structures

Commissions are set by the seller or the e-retailer. Some affiliates are paid a flat fee for each purchase that one of your customers makes, whereas with other affiliate programs, you're paid a percentage of the purchase price. The bottom line is that you can make money by promoting other people's products.

But you can also make money by creating a product and letting affiliates sell it for you. In that case, you would be making the lion's share of the money, and you would pay each affiliate for what they sold at your site. Fortunately for us, affiliate commissions are usually automatically calculated and paid to the affiliates, as explained when you signed up for the program.

The bonus of having your own product is that if you create information products such as an eBook, you can include affiliate links to other products or services that you feel the person reading the book would benefit from. Sometimes Internet Marketers will create a short report, package it as a PDF file, and then give it away on their website or blog.

Creating such a report can have a viral effect on the Internet, which means that whoever originally downloaded your free report can share it or give it away on their website or blog. Then every time someone reads your free giveaway book or report; your affiliate links are active. If someone clicks on a link and purchases, you get paid.

Most Internet Marketers are affiliates for products in addition to their own. Rather than talking to a friend on the phone and giving them a link to a specific site where they could buy something, you could just tell them you'll send them an email with the information. Then inside that email you would include your affiliate link to the site.

BLOGGING

A blog is a place on the web where the blog owner and web visitors can leave comments on anything that's been written. The word "blog" comes from "web log" which is a sort of journaling record or diary of thoughts and facts. To become interactive with the content displayed on a blog, users add their "comments" along with an email address and their name.

All comments can be seen by anyone unless the owner of the blog password protects a specific area, for example in a membership site. Leaving a comment on a blog with a link back to your website or blog is one way for obtaining backlinks, which essentially make your site look more popular, while making the blog appear as more of an authority. The more links coming into your site, the better.

For those who don't like to write, earning a side income as a "blogging" Internet Marketer might not be as popular with you as some of the other income streams. Keep in mind that if you're following someone's blog posts *(their journal entry for a specific day),* and you leave positive comments, and often, the blog owner will begin to see that your comments are genuine contributions to the blog itself.

Blogging, just like other social media avenues like Twitter or Facebook, encourage relationships and the sharing of information. While it's true that not every blog post is a positive one that gets written by a web visitor, many long-term business partnerships can branch out of blogging.

Another way to get more customers coming to your site is to see if the blog that you frequently visit uses guest contributors. If so, then you could write a meaty 750-1,000 word article about a topic of interest to that specific blog owner.

If your article gets accepted, the goal is a link back to your site and a "mention" as a guest contributor. The benefit is that all the visitors to that blog will have an opportunity to read your article and then follow the link to your site, or at least find out more about you. It requires time to write the article, and time to communicate with the blog owner, but other than that, there are no costs involved.

I like to think of my time spent blogging as a valid investment in my Internet Marketing business. It's free. I can blog whenever I have a few minutes, and it puts my website's link out there. There's nothing wrong with free advertising, right?

One Blog or Many?

Bloggers can make money by writing reviews about expensive products and then include a couple of affiliate links that take the reader to the site to read more and to purchase. It's been said that some successful bloggers earn a six-figure income just from writing little blog posts that talk about, recommend, or review online products.

Imagine if you had one blog that was making money that way, how much you could earn if you had a whole network of blogs. You probably would only need to update one blog about twice a month because your followers would eagerly read your latest posts based on their notification preferences.

BEWARE: This is another way to get addicted to the career of becoming an Internet Marketer. I said beware because it takes time to create a blog and update it. You can choose this income stream, but you'll need to pay attention to updating your blogs rather than just creating them and never tending to them.

How to Make Money with Your Blog

Many successful bloggers make a passive income every month through displaying Google AdSense ads on their blogs. Business owners who create ads using the Google Adwords advertising program can choose to have their ads shown on other businesses websites.

The way you make money is that when one of your site visitors clicks the link on an ad displayed on your site,

Google charges the advertiser, and then records that click in your account. You cannot click the ads that are displayed on your own site because it is against Google's rules.

Since Google owns one of the top search engines on the Internet, all you have to do is get approved by Google to display AdSense ads on your site. After that, you just need to put a small piece of code on your webpage or blog. When the Google ads are displayed on your site, based on a searcher's keywords, you get paid a few cents or a few dollars, depending on the price that Google assigns per click.

Sometimes the income you earn from one blog by having Google AdSense ads displayed on your site can easily pay for your domain name renewal and your website hosting for the year. Just make sure that your content reflects the keywords in the description of the page so that you can attract more traffic.

Another way to make money with your blog is to advertise an affiliate product through banner ads or links strategically placed inside of your content. You can also write reviews of a product and include your affiliate link.

The affiliate product that you choose to show to your customers should be in line with the nature of your blog. Some products are universal in nature and would appeal to the average consumer. However, if you're advertising the product that your customers can't relate to, you're most likely not going to make many sales. Yes, that is an assumption, but your goal as a blogger is to deliver information and products to your target audience that are very focused.

Of course, if you have already created your own product, then you will definitely want to prominently display a banner ad or an easy-to-see call-out that encourages people to click the link and buy your product.

Still other bloggers include a "Donate" button on their site, which allows people to give a blogger a tip or a monetary donation.

Blog Posting Frequency

If you're writing all your blog posts yourself, then aim for adding new posts twice a week. But don't make yourself crazy if one week you can only post one time. Life tasks and responsibilities sometimes don't allow enough time at the beginning of an Internet Marketer's career to frequently post an article during the week.

The search engines love new content and so do your web followers. It is not necessary to write a 750 word or 1,000 word blog post a couple of times a week. If you discover a shortcut that your readers would like to know about, then write a brief blog post of 250 words. Consistency and quality help build your brand as an Internet marketer.

To make your blog appear even more active, it's important for you to comment on the comments that your visitors are leaving at your site. People love attention. If they've left a genuine comment in appreciation for the article that you just posted, then thank them on the blog. If you've set your blog to using the WordPress platform, you can specify within your dashboard that you get notified every time someone leaves you a comment. Then once a day you can take 10 or 15 minutes to respond to one or more people's feedback.

Testing Your Ads

Blogging is a social platform. People like to interact with each other and with the owner of the blog if unique content is provided on a regular basis. Although it's not mandatory, if you are directing people to your blog through a mailing list, you might want to think about changing up any ads or banners on your site. It's a quick way to test your ads especially when there is a lot of communication on a specific blog post.

Testing just means that one day you use one banner ad and on the next day you use a different banner ad. At the end of a specific number of days, you might see more sales coming in from one ad over the other. Your testing then would tell you which ad your blog readers responded to more often; thereby making you more money.

BUYING TRAFFIC

Internet Marketers try many methods to get increased traffic to their sites, and sometimes they're willing to pay for that traffic. One of the leaders in Pay Per Click (PPC) advertising is Google. When you sign up for a Google Adwords account (PPC), you will be able to set a daily or monthly budget that will be reduced every time someone clicks one of your ads. The bonus to spending the money is that if you do it right, you can make a lot of money.

Buying traffic in the online world is similar to placing a classified ad in a newspaper or magazine. The advertising company will require that you pay in advance of when the ads will run. The same is true with Google Adwords. But unlike a print ad, when you pay your money and the ad runs with Adwords, you'll want to log into your account every day to check the results. If you're running successful ads, then the price of each click will help you analyze the conversion of how much money you're spending with Adwords versus how many sales you've made.

With print ads, you never know if anyone will read your ad. With PPC advertising, whenever a web surfer types a keyword phrase into their favorite search engine, your ad will be displayed—ready for visitors to click the ad and be immediately whisked off to your site to see what you're selling and for how much money.

Important to your Internet Marketing success is that once a visitor arrives at the front door of your site, that you're delivering what you've promised. If you're advertising a product or service and it's not obvious to the web visitor that you have what they're looking for, they'll leave.

That's called a bounce. When your site receives too many bounce results, it tells the search engines that users are not finding anything of interest to them at your site. Therefore, make sure your landing page or your home page is easy to navigate so people can find a solution to their query.

How to Tell When Your Ad Isn't Effective

The first indication that you might need to reword your ad or cancel or pause an ad is when you're not getting any sales compared to the money you're spending on every click. Ideally, you'll want to look at your competitors PPC ads that use the same or similar keywords as you do.

If they're ranking in the top three positions, then study their ads and see how you might want to modify yours to attract more clicks to your site. Just remember not to plagiarize someone else's ad by using the exact same words.

The length of time to determine whether your ad is effective or not depends upon your budget, your target audience, and what product or service you're promoting.

If you have a small or limited budget, then check to see how many clicks per day you'll get for that amount of money. Google Adwords has a lot of helpful guides and tutorials if you want to learn more about increasing your conversions. They also have a phone number that you can call and ask for help. Naturally, they won't tutor you, but they are willingly available to answer one or two questions that you have about your account.

MORE SITES EQUALS MORE MONEY?

There are many ways to build a website or blog, and successful Internet Marketers have more than one site. In fact, when multiple sites are built, each one can turn into its own income-producing hub for your big money site *(where you focus a large portion of your time).*

To have your own blog or website, you'll need a domain name, which is how your site is found. For example, amazon.com is a domain name. If you add www in front of the domain name and type it into your favorite search engine, you will be immediately taken to the Amazon website.

Get a Domain Name for Your Worldwide Internet Presence

Domain names are very inexpensive, and you can choose whatever domain registry company you want. A quick search on the Internet will give you a list of sites that you can visit to see how much they charge, according to your country's money system.

How do you choose a domain name?

People search for information, products, and services by using model numbers of products, brand names, or by search terms known as keywords. The more targeted your keywords are will mean the easier it is to find your site among the millions of sites on the web. Therefore, try to choose a domain name that begins with your primary keyword or keyword phrase. You have a better chance of getting more business by not putting any other words or numbers in front of your keyword.

For example, which of the following four domain names do you think would generate the most traffic:

FrankSmith.com,
FSPlumbing.com,
yorkshireplumbingrepairs.com,
or
123smithplumbing.com?

(Disclaimer: Domain names are hypothetical.)

Based on using a keyword phrase or a location-based keyword, the third domain name would have a tendency to qualify higher in the search engines because if anyone in Yorkshire was looking for a plumber, the name is easy to remember, and it contains exactly what a potential client is looking for.

Getting Your Domain Name onto the World Wide Web

Once you have your domain name, you need to pay for a hosting account where your domain name will reside.

You can pay monthly or on a yearly basis to get the best price. If you're unfamiliar with web hosting companies, you can do an Internet search for "web hosting companies." The majority of hosting companies have online tutorials, written or in video format, to walk you through the process of setting up your domain name. Just make sure that your hosting company displays your web information through a cPanel. A cPanel is site configuration and management software that allows users to visually control every aspect of their website and how it's hosted.

After you have your domain name and web hosting company, then it's time to build your site. Again, depending on your hosting company, most places have free website builders available that are point and click. That means that you do not have to know any programming or coding languages to create a website. Web design templates and programs are super simple to use and no prior experience is required. It's just up to you to decide on your favourite colors to use and the layout that will complement what you're selling.

The important thing to keep in mind is that you take action and build something to sell a product and to build a mailing list. You don't need to be a perfectionist before you can make your first sale.

Many Internet Marketers start with a small and simple site. After they've made several sales and their investment has already paid for itself, then they might want to hire a website designer to create a site with more bells and whistles. But again, that's not important. If you even have a one page sales letter with good copywriting, easy-to-follow directions on what you want your web visitor to do, and a payment button, you're good to go.

ARTICLE MARKETING

If you're good at writing, or if you have a good outsource writer, you can write articles and submit them to article directories with a link back to your own site. Many Internet Marketers use article marketing to promote various sites. These sites can be where you're an affiliate and you get a commission for every sale, or you can offer your web visitors more than just one product to purchase.

Articles can range from 250 words to 1,000 words. The average article is around 400 to 500 words. The goal is to provide enough useful information that someone would want to read your article and follow the link to the site that you're promoting.

Volumes of books and courses cover the strategies and techniques of writing creative articles that will attract people to your website. But one thing is for sure: content is needed for everything you do in Internet Marketing. If you start by writing a few articles and submit them to article directories, you will begin to see the amount of traffic that arrives just based on one article.

Whatever you do, don't ever copy someone else's article and put your name on it. That's illegal and it's called plagiarizing. When you're first getting started in Internet Marketing, to save money if you can write the articles yourself, and then later when you have made a few sales, you can buy some Private Label Rights (PLR) content or commission someone to write the articles for you. Just understand that you get what you pay for; after all, this is your new career and you should take care of it by providing unique content that no one else has seen before.

In addition to using the articles to promote your own website, you can make good extra income through your writing skills. It's one sure way to become a published writer. Write an article, have someone publish it, and there you are...a published author.

Making Money through Article Marketing

You can make money not only by submitting your articles to article directories and having someone buy your product once they arrive at your website. You can write articles and get paid for writing those articles. Many businesses on the Internet advertise that they're looking for writers. Just register at the site, follow their directions, and wait for approval.

Just think about making money on the Internet from the comfort of your home, a coffee shop, or anywhere in the world. You don't have to drive through traffic. You don't have to report to a boss. You can wear your comfy clothes and you can set your own hours.

Some Internet Marketers contact web developers and offer their services as a third-party vendor. This simply means that you would not be dealing directly with their clients. However, the web developer can build a website for a customer and give them the option of providing the content. When a web developer gets such an order, you are contacted and given the amount of content required, along with keyword phrases or titles for the pages. Again, you're helping the web developer, he's helping his client, he doesn't have to do the work, and you get paid.

If you have a team of writers who can write for you, you can take on more web developer clients. But your workers would not have access to the web developer, and you would be the gatekeeper to make sure that each article has been proofread and perfect before you send it to your client. Just remember to establish your deadlines with room for 50% flexibility. Things happen, and you need to build in a cushion of time so that you deliver your products in a timely manner.

It's fun to sit in front of your computer writing articles, knowing that you're going to make money!

There are many styles that you can choose from when you're writing articles. Some of the most popular are lists, for example, Five Ways to Save Money this Christmas. Or, 10 Steps to Freedom from Smoking. Another writing style uses bulleted lists, such as, Five Ways to Get Out of a Speeding Ticket:

- Do this

- Do this

- Do this

- Do this

- Do this

Another style is the three layer structure: in the first paragraph, tell them what you're going to tell them. In the second paragraph provide the information. In the third paragraph, tell them what you just told them and list a few benefits.

As you begin reading various articles on the Internet, you will discover many styles and formats for writing an article. Choose a few methods and then write a batch of five articles according to one of those styles. It makes article writing easier when you have a plan and a system.

Remember, every article should have a beginning, middle, and an end, just like every newspaper article, every book, every blog post, and every piece of web content on your website.

SEARCH ENGINE OPTIMIZATION (SEO)

Search engine optimization, or as it is known in the industry, SEO, gets many Internet Marketers so excited. Why? When your website is set up in such a manner that it goes from not being found on the Internet to appearing on the first page of the search engines, such as Google, Yahoo, and Bing, it means that you are going to make more money because people will find your listing before they find anyone else's.

Internet Marketers whose websites appear on the first page of Google have the potential to make thousands of dollars every day. Of course, it depends what you're selling and if your website delivers what the link promises.

SEO is also known as a method for ranking high in what's called organic search. That means as long as your website contains all of the elements that attract buyers and your website is SEO compliant for the search engines, you don't have to pay any money to rank on the first page of Google. It's an organic search as opposed to PPC or paid advertising.

If you're building a website with an SEO focus, you must provide value to your web visitor with the content you provide. If you follow all of the SEO rules, and you have little to no content, or your content is poorly written and offers no value to the customer, you might rank high in the search engines for a day or two, but when your site is indexed *(re-evaluated and re-ranked)* by the search engine spiders, your listing will drop off of page one.

MOST IMPORTANT: Before you attempt to make money in this niche of Internet Marketing, it's best if you have mastered SEO practices on your own website and have ranked on page one of Google. It will be easier to sell services when you can show your customer that your website is on page one.

How to Make Money with SEO

There are several ways to make money with SEO. You can offer your services to webmasters who build sites for their customers. You can build a site in a niche market that has attained a page one ranking and you can rent that niche site for one year. Likewise, you can build a site, get it ranked on page one, and then sell it.

Many Internet Marketers understand that a large portion of work depends on finding the best keywords and keyword phrases with the least amount of competition. They create lists of niche related keywords within a specific market and then they sell those keyword lists to fellow Internet Marketers. You might wonder why an Internet Marketer would not do their own keyword research. The quick answer is that it takes time and expertise along with research to create the targeted keyword lists.

Internet Marketers making lots of money try to outsource as many tasks as possible so they can refocus their efforts on marketing and getting more clients, which means more money in their bank account.

People are willing to pay good money to get ranked on the first page of Google. But it's a lot of hard work and if you are an SEO expert you will need to stay current with all the latest trends and news that involve changes to how websites are ranked. However there is lots of money to be made in this marketplace.

Tip: Internet Marketers have to pick and choose what they want to do, since they can't be a jack of all trades. Do what you like to do and then outsource the rest.

If your website is properly optimized, and you do get a page one ranking, then you need to continue to build backlinks to your website and provide fresh content for your visitors. The goal is to try to keep your web traffic on your website looking at videos, listening to audio and reading content. Those are several of the elements that indicate to the search engines that your site is an authority site because people spend more than one minute looking around.

If you're interested in learning more about search engine optimization, there is a lot of free information on the web.

Just make sure that the site you're accessing is an authority site as well. You need to be able to trust the information they give you in order to obtain a page one ranking on the search engines. The best thing to do is to try one or two tactics on your own website and see if you go from not being found to page 100, and then to page 10, and ideally to page one.

Through this process you will learn what works and what not to spend your time on. If you enjoyed this type of research and implementation, then you can make some good money. If it takes you too much time and you don't like doing your own SEO work, then hire somebody to do it for you.

When you're working in the comfort of your own home and doing what you love, you will find more ways to continue to make money in your Internet Marketing career. The payoff to continue working at your full-time job while still beginning and maintaining your part-time Internet Marketing job is worth it when you discover that you can make a good living by working on your own.

Not every Internet Marketer chooses one income stream and then two months later quits their full-time job. Just like any other career, it might appear that someone became a millionaire in the Internet Marketing business and it seemed like it happened overnight. But most likely it didn't. Just remember not to give up.

Start small, keep your budget in mind before buying anything, and set a goal for yourself, like: this month I want to make $100 from my Internet Marketing business. You can set whatever goal you want; just make sure that it's realistic so you don't get discouraged.

Some Internet Marketers started with a goal of earning enough money in one month to pay their car payment. Think what that would mean to you if you knew that your Internet Marketing business could make enough money to do that.

BACKLINK SERVICE

Backlinks are incoming links to a website or web page. When a link from an authority site links to your site, it is said that your site is given more value from the search engines. As an Internet Marketer you can locate sites that will allow you to drop a web link back to your site, or you can hire someone to do the backlinking service for you.

You might be wondering where you would find websites that would allow you to include a link back to your own website. Most forums allow you to register and become one of their members. Depending on that forum's rules, you will be able to create a signature line and even add a URL back to your website. When the search engines see that someone is linking to your site from another site that is given more value than if you didn't have any backlinks.

You could accumulate hundreds or thousands of backlinks to your website, because that looks natural and organic in the world of search engines. If thousands of website owners are linking to your site it means that you must have some information, a product, or a service that other people want to remember; plus, the backlink.

Two types of backlinks that Google really loves are when you get a link from an .edu or .gov website. One such backlink is easily equivalent to 2,000 regular forum or blog links. Internet Marketers are willing to spend money to get a handful of these golden backlinks because it pushes their site closer to page one of the search engines.

Many marketers are skeptical about buying backlinks because they think it will somehow ruin their website's ranking. As long as the backlinks are being built in what appears to be a normal amount of time, then you can stay under the radar. For example, it would not appear natural to the search engines if you suddenly had 20,000 people linking to your website for no apparent reason.

Certainly, if you were involved in something that was hugely newsworthy in your state, or in your country, and every news channel and radio announcer was talking about it, then yes, you would receive an increased amount of traffic from outside web links. But that's not normal.

How to Make Money by Offering a Backlink Service

You can make money by locating the sites that will accept a backlink and selling that list to other Internet Marketers on a monthly and recurring basis. The second way to make money would be to hire outsourcers who would actually register at each one of the sites and place a link, a username, and a short bio for your customers.

Then you could sell a backlink service that would create the backlinks. Naturally you would have to charge more than what you would pay your outsourcer, but you basically become the middleman. This is also easily put onto a recurring basis if they are already buying your backlink site package.

Various programmers have created software that will locate sites for you that will accept backlinks. Again, remember to stay within your budget, and to only choose those revenue streams that you can be utterly passionate about every day that you wake up knowing that that's what you'll be doing that day.

Have you decided yet if Internet Marketing sounds like something you would like to do? For me, I'm passionate about a lot of things so I'm always looking for new ways to add a revenue stream to my business. I would rather be working at my business than watching television or taking a nap.

Yes, I'm an Internet Marketing addict!

EBAY

Some Internet Marketers believe that eBay is in the category of Internet Marketing, whereas some people don't consider eBay as a way to make a six-figure income per year. That's probably because they've never tried it or been successful at it. I'm not talking about looking in your attic or garage to see if you have something that instead of throwing in the trash you can put for sale on eBay. I'm talking about a full-blown store and business that you operate on eBay.

What I've found is that eBay offers a way to sell information products *(eBooks & Videos etc. on a CD rom)* and when someone is looking for a specific topic that I ready have a captive audience built-in. EBay shoppers come to the site to buy things. Their credit cards are handy. When they search in a specific category where they have an interest, and they see your product, eBay makes it very easy for them to buy it.

Sales are handled through eBay auctions or Classified ads. You create a one-page sales letter on their site, upload a couple of photos, add a description, fill-in the required information to have someone complete the sale, and you go live with your listing.

Make Money with eBay's Affiliate Program

EBay also has an affiliate program. That means if someone sees that your products are selling well, they could set up an affiliate link to promote your product so they get paid. But you get paid, too.

EBay pays its affiliates whenever you send someone to their site and your customer makes a purchase. That's why you might have seen many sites on the Internet that give a product review or mention something in a niche market with a link that connects to their auction or product on eBay. Or, they might provide a link to another eBay store as an affiliate, knowing that they're going to make money off of that site every month.

EBay does have charges for listing an auction on their website, and for placing a Classified Ad, even if your product doesn't sell. When your product does sell, they take a portion of the final sale. The best part about eBay is that you begin to understand how to make the most sales from the products you offer.

You can also look at how other store owners and eBay sellers create their pages and advertise their products. Again, don't copy verbatim what they have done, but use one of their pages as a template or example for you to try when selling your product.

Getting approved for the eBay affiliate program can be quite difficult, but you can find courses on the Internet that will reveal exactly what you need to do to get approved.

The key to making money as an Internet Marketer is to create relationships with people and other sites. You need to get known in the advertising world for all the effort you're putting into profiting in your new career. If no one knows about you, and they can't find your site, you'll have to do more advertising to make sales.

BUILDING AND SELLING WEBSITES

Another income stream that always seems to be in demand is building websites for business owners or hobbyists. If you have created your own website using static HTML, a WYSIWYG website designer *program (what you see is what you get)*, or if you have developed a site using Joomla, Drupal, or WordPress, and you love creating websites, you can make a great living by selling and building websites for other people.

When the demand for your website building services has more orders coming in during a one-month period then you can easily crank out by yourself, then you can outsource some of the web building tasks. Many website developers create a series of templates that they sell. Some templates are in a general business category, whereas other templates are uniquely focused to a specific niche.

You can specialize in one niche and go after all of those types of businesses. Or, you can offer three levels of website creation services, such as a basic five-page website, a one-page sales letter site, a video opt-in site, an intermediate site, or a custom-built site.

The prices that you could charge vary from $350-$5000 for one site, depending upon what your customer wants.

And don't forget, every new website will need content, SEO, backlinks, and an array of other services such as graphics, logos, and videos. Building one website is just the gateway to selling many other services.

How to Make Money Building, Renting, and Selling Websites

Internet Marketers can make money first by building their own sites to use as an example. You can offer your services to build websites for clients. You can build spec websites, get them ranked, add some content, and flip the website. Flipping a website means that you're more interested in building the site, adding value to it, and selling it to another Internet Marketer. Needless to say, that website that you would flip and sell for lots of money will include the domain name.

You can be the so-called storefront. Your website advertises the fact that you build websites for people. You talk to the customer, they fill out a form telling you what they want, and then instead of you building it, you can have an outsourcer build the website for you. You work directly with your client and the outsourcer. You make the money, and you pay your outsourcer.

A general guideline is that you will charge twice as much as it will cost you to have your outsourcer create the site. Make sure that your customer understands your process and the length of time it will take.

It's best if you choose an outsourcer who has a good reputation for delivering what you want and on time. For your own protection, always build in two extra weeks to the timeline of when you will have the website completed for your client, just in case your outsourcer doesn't produce.

By the way, if you are going through a service that employs hundreds of freelancers, be forewarned not to pay for this service in advance. The web design outsourcer must create the website to your satisfaction before you will pay that person.

In business, even when you do find a web developer who you can use to build the websites for you for your customers, it's always good to have someone as a backup person. Let's say that you sell five websites a month. You would give two projects to one developer and three projects to the other developer. In other words, you're never relying on just one person.

Remember, your reputation is what sets you apart from other businesses. When you build websites to your customer's satisfaction and within the timeframe that you promised that it would be completed, and you have a fair price, you will get repeat business. But if you promised to deliver a website and your outsourcer fails to deliver, it's imperative that you have a backup person to jump in as needed to build that site within the timeframe you specified to your client.

If you decide to build websites and either rent them to niche market players or you choose to build the site and flip it for money, here are some pricing guidelines to consider. Let's say that one site earns five dollars a day. That equals $150 a month. For someone who is interested in buying your site, you could easily charge $1,000. It's simple to see how you can definitely make a substantial part-time income from building, selling, renting, or flipping websites.

Renting a website means that you have built a niche market site with a powerful domain name and you're getting traffic to the site. Once you have obtained a good sales record and rank for your site on the search engines result pages, you can approach local businesses and inquire if they would like to rent your website for one year.

Why would they want to do this?

Some business owners are not making any money off of their website, or they haven't been able to achieve page one rankings on Google. If you show them one website that you have already built and that is bringing in income, all you have to do is change their contact information in the mail of their business and they can start earning money off of that website. It's valuable money for you and the client doesn't have to wait for the site to be built. Plus, you're the owner of the site. Maybe you can charge for maintenance.

As long as the client renting your site continues to renew their monthly or yearly payment with you, then you've just created a passive income revenue stream. If that works for you, then build more sites and rent them, or sell them.

PRIVATE LABEL RIGHTS (PLR)

Private Label Rights (PLR) is a term that means once you purchase a product that offers PLR rights, depending on who is selling the package, you will be allowed to put your name as the author of the product, you can change the title, you can change any of the information inside the PLR product, and you can sell it at any price you wish.

The beauty of PLR products is that someone else has done all the work for you, which can save you a lot of time in your Internet Marketing business.

Customers can purchase your PLR product, and if it is an eBook, they can turn right around and sell it as is. But if you are selling PLR articles, then the purchaser needs to rewrite each article so that it is unique and not a duplicate of the original article.

You might be asking yourself why you would buy a PLR product if you have to do all the work and rewrite the articles yourself. The short answer is that most articles are priced around one dollar per article, since the seller will sell multiple copies of the same content. Therefore, to make sure that the articles that you will use on your website, blog, or submit to article directories are unique; you will need to rewrite the content.

On the other hand, if you were to commission someone to write five articles for you, rather than paying five dollars for the five PLR articles, you might have to pay anywhere from $10-$25 or more just for one article.

How to Make Money as A PLR Marketer

Many Internet Marketers hire one or more writers to create five articles at a time that all pertain to the same topic. When you outsource this type of work, the writer for hire will give you either a flat rate fee or a per word fee. For example, you might pay $10 for a 500 word article, so for five articles, it would cost you $50. But you could turn around and sell a five pack of PLR articles for five dollars. All you would need to sell is 10 packs and you will have recouped your investment. Thereafter, every sale is sheer profit.

This is easily calculated if your outsource writer charges by the word rather than assessing a flat fee. In the example above, a 500 word article priced at two cents per word would cost you $10.

The best advice is to make sure that you hire a native English speaking writer. Many other tasks can be outsourced, but anyone who uses English as their primary language will quickly figure out that an article was not written by an English-speaking writer.

Various Internet Marketers do not require a membership site for clients to buy their PLR article packs. However there are others who only sell their PLR articles, eBooks, and autoresponder messages through a membership site.

A membership site requires that the customer pay a monthly fee to gain access to the PLR products that are produced each month inside the member's area.

One final note is that if you can quickly write articles, especially SEO articles, then you would not have to pay an outsourcer. Imagine if you could write 10 articles per day, which would be the equivalent of two 5-packs. Those 10 articles would sell for $10. Now imagine if you wrote 10 articles per day for 20 days out of every month. How many articles would you have to sell? The answer is 200. Okay so let's say that you could only create five articles per day for 20 days out of the month. That means that you would have created 100 PLR articles that you could easily sell on your website.

Do you see the potential here as a revenue stream? In addition, if you belong to any type of Internet Marketing forum, you could sell these PLR article packs quite easily either through a special offer, as a PLR rating service, through a classified ad, or by including a link in your signature line to your PLR website. Think about it.

SELLING PAID PER CLICK (PPC) SERVICES

Another way that Internet marketers make a great deal of money, even six-figure incomes per year, is through offering to manage a business's Google Adwords PPC program. Setting up PPC campaigns and writing ads is very simple and can bring unbelievable amounts of income to your client who is willing to pay you on a reoccurring monthly basis to manage their PPC campaigns, along with a budget that you suggest to them.

PPC stands for pay-per-click. When you type in a series of keywords or a keyword phrase into your favorite search engine, when you look at the results pages, you will notice that the top ads and ads on the side are sponsored ads. What this means is that someone has paid to advertise their business through a PPC program.

The majority of business owners are not well-versed in managing their PPC campaigns or their ads. That's where you come in. You can set up the campaign for them. You can create the ads for them. The only prerequisite you have is that they pay you in advance for the services that you will perform throughout the month.

What Does Your Client Care About When They Hire You?

All the client cares about is their conversion rates and that they make money; not lose it. In other words, if they are paying you $250 a month to maintain their PPC campaign and they have a $1,000 a month advertising budget, they need to realize a profit greater than what your monthly fee is and that's where you can make a killing.

This income stream is not for the faint of heart. You must have already set up your own Google Adwords PPC campaign, set a budget, and made a profit. If you can do this once, you can do this for any client. Why? As previously stated, most business owners have set up their PPC accounts incorrectly and they're basically throwing money out the window. You become their hero when you go in and turn everything around and they start earning more money.

<u>TIP</u>: Don't run after your client every month to get your recurring fee. Do your research, and set up an account with a Direct Debit Provider. How it works is that your client allows a direct debit to come out of their bank account every month for your fee and the PPC budget. This amount of money is deposited into your account so that you can manage the client's PPC campaign. If your client refuses to do business with you this way, then dismiss the client and thank them for their

time. Believe me; it is not worth your time or effort contacting every client every month to get your money and the budgeted money that the client wants to spend in their PPC campaign.

MOBILE MARKETING FOR OFFLINE BUSINESS OWNERS

Mobile marketing means two things to Internet Marketers: more and more clients arrive at your website every day through the use of their mobile phone; if your website is not mobile ready, then you're losing traffic and sales.

Internet marketers can approach any business owner and let them know that their website is not mobile compatible. Therefore, you're not offering to sell anything, but you're just telling him that the mobile market is increasing by the thousands every month. Even banks encourage mobile users to do their banking through their mobile phones. Customers search for businesses that will take their money and to do that you need to have a mobile ready website.

What is an offline business?

An offline business is a physical retail store or business that advertises through the Internet. Their sales are generally made through their physical store location. They will spend massive amounts of money on advertising to bring customers through their doors. Yet, if they don't have a website, you can sell them one by building it for them. However, if they already have a web presence, and their site is not mobile compatible, they are losing a lot of money.

How to Sell Mobile Marketing Services to Offline Businesses

Mobile marketing may seem like a new concept for many people who are not familiar with it or they don't follow the latest technological trends. However, the mobile market accounts for

20- 30 percent of online sales. It's projected that sales via mobile phones will increase by as much as 50 percent within the next two years. Even in countries that are in remote locations, the majority of residents own mobile phones.

Yellow page advertising doesn't work anymore because the world has turned to social media as a way of communicating and doing business. Let's say that a business in the town where you live, such as a pizza restaurant, a clothing store, a plumbing business, or a chiropractor wants to increase their sales and get more customers into their store buying products and services. Mobile marketing is what will take them to the next level.

As an Internet Marketer, you can create QR codes that can easily be scanned from any mobile phone to give a potential customer a discount, a phone number to call, or any other bonus the business owner wants to offer. You, as the Internet Marketer offering mobile marketing services, are their direct link to making money in this shrinking economy.

The first place to start is to make the offline business owner's website mobile compatible. They pay you to do this. The next step is to offer QR codes. After that, you could have them offer discount coupons online. The next step is to set up an opt-in form on their website so that the business owner can do a blast announcement of special discounts for that day by entering a code. There are many opportunities within this business niche.

How do you get started in making money with mobile marketing to offline businesses?

Do a search for any type of business in the city where you live. Look at their website, use your mobile phone, and see if it is a mobile compatible site. I guarantee you that most websites will not have mobile compatibility.

Send a quick email to the business owner letting them know that you tried to access their website with your mobile phone but you couldn't place an order. Or, if you're okay with in-person sales, stop in at the business and ask for the owner.

If the owner is present, tell him that you couldn't access his website from your mobile phone, but you can give him a solution. If the owner is not there, leave your business card, and ask the owner to call if he wants to get more customers coming through his door with mobile marketing.

As an incentive, and this is totally up to you as the Internet Marketer, tell the business owner that you will only set up one mobile marketing campaign in their ZIP/Post code. But you've already made your offer to five other businesses. If the owner is interested in speaking with you, ask that person to call you.

That might sound like a scarcity tactic, but you're interested in bringing the offline business owner information that they need. You're not going to offer the service to every pizza place in town. You're going to select one and present your offer to that person. If the business owner declines, then you're free to approach another pizza place.

As with many other Internet Marketing income streams, you can find a variety of courses and downloadable information that will tell you how to approach an offline business with mobile marketing services. The bonus for you is that right now not many marketers are doing this, so this is your opportunity to get in with a ground-floor strategy. Take over your little town and any other towns within 50 miles of where you live. Go for it!

THE TOP FIVE INTERNET MARKETING MISTAKES TO AVOID

This book would not be complete without me telling you about the Internet marketing mistakes that you should avoid. I want you to be successful. I want you to become an Internet marketing addict just like I am, but I don't want you to fail before you get started.

A lot of information has been provided in this book, and you may have to read through it several times before you decide which income stream you would like to pursue. However, I just want to remind you one more time about how much I love my career as an Internet marketer. I want you to succeed.

Listed below are the top five Internet Marketing mistakes to avoid.

1. **If you decide to market your services through email, the best thing you can do for your business and yourself is to be totally honest**. By being truthful and not sounding like a paid script, the recipients of your messages will feel your honesty and integrity to helping them succeed. If your email reads like a form letter, the

person reading it will just hit delete. Remember, you're not just selling. You're educating your customer. By creating a relationship based on trust and honesty, you should create an atmosphere that gives your potential client the confidence to approach you with any questions, free of charge. Convey that to them. Don't be afraid to give them your opinion when they ask you for it. Remember, you're the expert and you want to bring them more business.

2. **Do not, I repeat, do not promote just one product**. Not every business owner will fit into a stereotypical box, and certainly, no one likes to be sold to. If you're advertising your services through online classified ads, don't use the same text in every single ad. Give the viewer a reason to click on your ad and to see what you're offering. If you use the same ad repeatedly, they won't read about what you're offering.

3. **Make sure you understand the difference between passive revenue and active streams of income**. Even though you yearn to break out of your 9-to-5 job, the income you're earning is active. In most instances you know exactly what you're going to make every week or every month at your J.O.B. Passive revenue, however, means that you create a product once or a website once and you continue to make money

off of that effort that you put into that income stream for an unlimited amount of time.

4. **Mistake number four is when you use your charge card to buy every product that appears in your Inbox**. As Internet marketers, we call this being attracted to the shiny object. Don't become attracted to the shiny object! Every offer that you hear about or read about promises to take you from zero to a six-figure income, but it's their success, not yours. Don't fall for the marketing hype. Don't spend your money buying offer after offer and not implementing anything. What works for one Internet marketer might not work for you. Be forewarned. Choose one revenue stream, put in your time, launch it, and make it work. Then choose another revenue stream. But don't quit your day time job until you're absolutely sure that you can support yourself or your family with a consistent income.

5. **Don't just read this book and put it on the shelf**. My final advice to you is to take action today while you're reading this book. Take a sheet of paper and write down five things you think you could implement within the next month that you read about in this book or that you think you would have a passion for in the future. Then create a step-by-step plan for accomplishing your goals.

CONCLUSION

Yes, as I said at the beginning of this book, I am addicted to Internet Marketing. I love helping people achieve their dreams, and I love earning an income from the comfort of my home wearing my most comfortable clothes. I don't live for money. But I do want a better life for myself and my family. I hope you do, too. Working as an Internet Marketer is very rewarding in more ways than just the money that comes into my bank account.

Instead of saying to yourself that you're going to "try" becoming an Internet Marketer, make a commitment. Take action. Make plans. Even if you work only several hours a week on your Internet Marketing business, one day you'll make that first sale, and then another, and another.

I believe in you, and I know that if you just put forth your best efforts that you can make money selling on the Internet. All you need is to believe in yourself and take action. One year from now you could be in a totally different place with your career.

What's stopping you? Are you ready to get started?

ABOUT THE AUTHOR

I'm Randolf Smith, friends call me Randy ☺

I've already confessed to being addicted to Internet Marketing. I own and operate several websites some of which are detailed on my own blog at www.RandolfSmith.com

I've been 'working' online since 2000 and been making a regular income since late 2005.
(Yep plenty of years of failure, or did I mean learning experiences, before I got serious).

I use to term 'work' loosely - as I'm all for leading a passionate life.
I've done the 100 hour weeks and believe me they're no fun. So now I figure I work to enjoy life, and therefore only do things I enjoy and am passionate about.

I'll say upfront - I'm no super star guru or millionaire! But I do know what I know and I hope that my products help you learn what you need to know to move yourself to new levels in your online adventures.

I won't give you a full life story.... it would hardly be relevant, and just fill pages with boring details you don't want to know ... *(smile)* What is relevant is my career history.

My background offline was of over twenty years in direct sales & marketing.

I have 4 daughters from my first marriage who've left home, and I'm currently engaged to my Beautiful Ray of Sunshine, Rachel. We've been together since 2008.

I've built my online income purely from the profits it has generated, and even that has been slower than I would have wished, though now it could be said I'm quite accomplished at Internet Marketing, I have had my share of failures.
I did get to a point where I owned my own offline business, but that eventually lead to bankruptcy with the recession that the whole world seems to be facing.

Thankfully I focused on my 'hobby' of Internet Marketing, and that lead me to a place where I work when I want to and enjoy more free time that I ever have in my previous careers.
Therefore it's my goal to share my knowledge and experiences with my subscribers and readers to help them get to a point where they too can enjoy life and what they do to make a living!

My best piece of advice would always be to take it steady "Step by Step" serve your apprenticeship and I know you'll get there :)

And do remember:
The way to eat an Elephant.....

Is one bite at a time!

If you want to know more you know where to find me :) My Websites....Well some of them are listed on my blog at: http://www.RandolfSmith.com

By Visiting I hope you'll subscribe to my mailing list and grab some of the free tools and reports that might guide you to what you need to learn in order to fulfill your own online goals ☺

My Favorite Saying
 Life: - Live it, Love it, Pass On The Passion!

I look forward to seeing you online, Addicted to Internet Marketing too ☺

www.ingramcontent.com/pod-product-compliance
Lightning Source LLC
Chambersburg PA
CBHW051344170526
45166CB00002B/953